Extraordinary Lives

WILLIAM SHAKESPEARE

Peter Hicks

Published in 2013 by Wayland
Copyright © Wayland 2013

Wayland
338 Euston Road
London NW1 3BH

Wayland Australia
Level 17/207 Kent Street
Sydney NSW 2000

Editor: Katie Powell
Designer: Phipps Design
Picture Researcher: Shelley Noronha

British Library Cataloguing in Publication Data
Hicks, Peter, 1952
William Shakespeare. – (Extraordinary lives)
1. Shakespeare,William, 1564-1616–Biography–Juvenile literature.
2.Dramatists, English–Early modern and Elizabethan, 1500-1600–Biography
–Juvenile literature.
I.Title II. Series
822.3'3-dc22

ISBN: 978 0 7502 7953 6

10 9 8 7 6 5 4 3 2 1

Picture acknowledgements: Cover © After John Vanderbank / Getty Images, p4 © The Art
Archive / British Museum / Eileen Tweedy, p5 © Wayland, artwork by Richard Hook,
p6 © Peter Hicks, p7 © Wayland, p8 © Peter Hicks, p9 © British Library, London,UK /
British Library Board.All Rights Reserved / The Bridgeman Art Library, p10 © Private
Collection / The Stapleton Collection / The Bridgeman Art Library, p11 © Peter Hicks,
p12 © The Art Archive / Eileen Tweedy, p13 © The Art Archive, p14 © Peter Hicks,
p15 © The Art Archive, p16 © Dulwich Picture Gallery, London,UK / The Bridgeman Art
Library, p17 © The Art Archive / Collection Comedie Francaise Paris / Laurie Platt Winfrey,
p18 © Peter Hicks, p19 © Belvoir Castle, Leicestershire, UK / The Bridgeman Art Library,
p20 © After John Vanderbank/ Getty Images, P21 © iStock, p22 © The Art Archive,
p23 © The Art Archive / British Library, p24 © The Art Archive / Museo del Prado Madrid /
Alfredo Dagli Orti, p25 © Peter Hicks, p26 © Rex Features Ltd, p27 iStock.
Every effort has been made to clear copyright. Should there be any inadvertent omission,
please apply to the publisher for rectification.

Printed in China

Wayland is a division of Hachette Children's Books,
an Hachette UK company.
www.hachette.co.uk First published in 2010 by Wayland

Contents

Words that appear in **bold** can be found in the glossary.

William Shakespeare – an extraordinary writer

December 1598 and the *Chamberlain's Men*, a successful **troupe** of actors, were in trouble! Their landlord, Giles Allen, was refusing to continue renting them the *Theatre* playhouse in London. The group tried to open an indoor theatre in Blackfriars but the **City fathers** banned the performance of plays.

A plot is formed

Although Giles Allen owned the land, the structure of the *Theatre* belonged to its builder, James Burbage, whose son, Richard was the head of the *Chamberlain's Men*. James died in February 1597, so his sons, Richard and Cuthbert, came up with a cunning plan.

This 18th century watercolour shows how the *Globe* theatre on the south bank of the Thames at Southwark might have looked during Shakespeare's time.

The men found a plot of land on the south bank of the River Thames, outside the control of the City fathers. Richard asked five of his fellow actors to invest £70 in the new theatre. These men included the poet and playwright William Shakespeare.

Taking action

The men had to act quickly. Giles Allen was going to destroy the *Theatre* and use the timber for himself. Under the cover of darkness on 28 December, the actors, a carpenter and a group of labourers met at the *Theatre*. They dismantled its timbers and ferried them across the Thames to the south bank. It was so cold they were able to slide them across the frozen river!

By 1598, William Shakespeare was a popular and respected poet and playwright with at least 19 plays to his name.

William Shakespeare had taken a massive risk – he might have ended up in prison! But he now owned part of a new theatre, for the *Globe* theatre was ready by the summer of 1599. With talented actors performing his plays, Shakespeare would make a small fortune!

Childhood and education

Legend says that William Shakespeare was born on 23 April 1564, but we can't be sure. We only know the date of Shakespeare's baptism, which was on 26 April 1564. He was the third child of John and Mary Shakespeare and was born in Henley Street, Stratford-upon-Avon.

Shakespeare's parents

Shakespeare's father made leather gloves and had a shop at the front of his house in Henley Street. John also **traded** in barley and wool, and lent money, helping him to become a rich man. Shakespeare's mother, Mary Arden, came from a wealthy farming family in the nearby village of Wilmcote.

Today, Shakespeare's family home in Henley Street, is a museum of his life and work.

Schooling

Shakespeare would have started school at four or five years old, in what was called a **petty school**. He would have learned the alphabet, small and capital letters, the Lord's Prayer, and the **Catechism**.

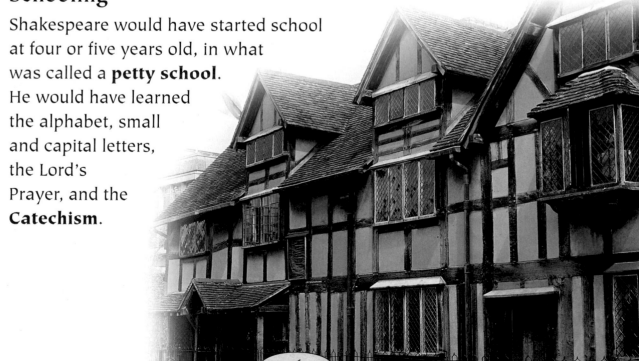

William Shakespeare's family tree

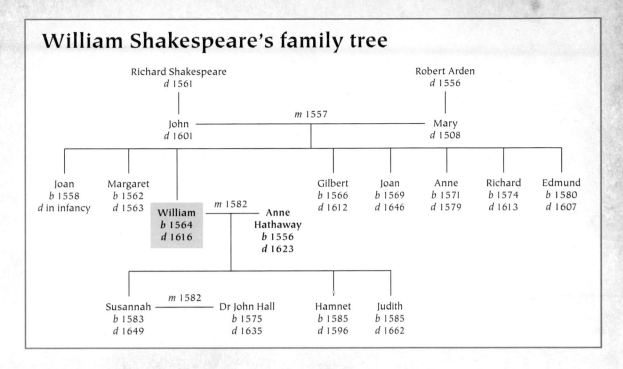

The following information is shown in the family tree:

Richard Shakespeare
d 1561

Robert Arden
d 1556

John — m 1557 — Mary
d 1601 — d 1508

Joan
b 1558
d in infancy

Margaret
b 1562
d 1563

William — m 1582 — Anne Hathaway
b 1564 — b 1556
d 1616 — d 1623

Gilbert
b 1566
d 1612

Joan
b 1569
d 1646

Anne
b 1571
d 1579

Richard
b 1574
d 1613

Edmund
b 1580
d 1607

Susannah — m 1582 — Dr John Hall
b 1583 — b 1575
d 1649 — d 1635

Hamnet
b 1585
d 1596

Judith
b 1585
d 1662

The Catechism was a series of questions and answers about the Christian faith that had to be learned. After two years at the petty school, Shakespeare would have gone to **grammar school**.

The school day was long in the 16th century. Latin, literature, poetry and history were drummed into Shakespeare from six in the summer or seven in the winter until five in the afternoon. Boys who didn't learn their lessons, speak Latin or behave politely were beaten with a leather strap by the master!

William never knew his older sisters and he outlived all but one of his younger brothers and sisters.

AGAINST THE ODDS

It is remarkable that Shakespeare survived his infancy, as only one in five babies survived their first month in 16th century England. Three months after Shakespeare's birth, the **plague** reached Stratford killing 237 people, more than 10 per cent of the town's population. A family of four, who lived on the same side of the street as Shakespeare, all died.

Stratford-upon-Avon

The place where Shakespeare grew up was a thriving **market town** on the River Avon. Sir Hugh Clopton's attractive bridge, built in the 1490s, still carries traffic over the river today. The town was small in Shakespeare's time, with about 2,000 inhabitants.

A town of prosperity

Stratford's **prosperity** could be seen in some of its impressive buildings, such as the Guild chapel and the beautiful church where Shakespeare was baptised. It was only a hundred miles from London and close to other important towns, such as Warwick, Coventry, Worcester and Oxford. Roads met at Stratford, bringing travellers, who often bought or sold goods.

The bridge over the River Avon was an important link with London when it was built in the 1490s.

William Shakespeare would have certainly witnessed travelling players, such as these, perform during his childhood.

Travelling players

John Shakespeare, Shakespeare's father, made his money from trade and he went on to become an important town official. In 1565, he became an **alderman** and then, in 1568, bailiff or mayor. This allowed him to use the town's money to invite troupes of travelling actors to perform in Stratford.

In 1569, troupes played in the town's **inn-yards**. John Shakespeare also invited the *Queen's Men* and the *Earl of Worcester's Men* to perform and, by the 1570s, Stratford was a popular place for visiting actors.

INSPIRATION

It's not difficult to imagine the young Shakespeare watching these plays and being dazzled by the colour and excitement. With his father as mayor, these troupes probably performed privately for the family at Henley Street, and it may have been where Shakespeare first fell in love with the theatre.

The 'lost' years

Shakespeare probably left grammar school at the age of 15. At this time, many boys would have gone on to university, but he chose not to, perhaps due to the family's financial hardship. Instead, he may have become his father's **apprentice** and learned the glove making trade.

Anne Hathaway was eight years older than Shakespeare. Here are the couple with two of their children, Judith and Susanna.

A man of mystery

Some historians believe Shakespeare worked in a lawyer's office as a clerk or became a teacher in Lancashire. Other writers claim he became a sailor or a soldier and went overseas. The time between leaving school and 1592, when we know for sure he was in London, are often called the 'lost' years.

One thing we know for certain during this time is that he started a family. In November 1582, at the age of 18, Shakespeare married 26-year-old Anne Hathaway.

Anne came from the nearby village of Shottery and was the daughter of a wealthy farmer. The couple had a daughter, Susanna, who was born in May 1583, followed by twins, Judith and Hamnet, in February 1585.

London bound

At some point after the birth of the twins, William left Stratford for London. There is a legend that says he fled there after being caught stealing deer! But it's more likely that he joined a troupe of actors and began his career in the theatre. We know that, in June 1587, the *Queen's Men* were touring Oxfordshire. While at Thame in Oxfordshire, two actors quarrelled and William Knell was killed in the fight. The troupe reached Stratford a man short. Did Shakespeare ask to join them? If this is what happened, it allowed a young, hopeful actor to go to London and learn his trade.

The house where Anne grew up is called Hewland Farm, but it is known today as 'Anne Hathaway's cottage'.

Shakespeare in London

It is thought that Shakespeare was living in London by 1588-89. He joined the 200,000 people living in and around its City walls. The River Thames was its southern boundary and its main 'highway'. Taxi-boats took people along the river.

Newcomer

The noise, smells and filth of London would have probably shocked Shakespeare. Although the Strand and Cheapside were proper roads, London's side-streets and alleys were muddy tracks littered with rubbish, including **sewage**, thrown from people's houses.

Shakespeare probably first lived in Shoreditch, near the theatre 'crowd'. Shoreditch was a violent area and Shakespeare may have carried a sword for protection. Many actors and **playwrights** died in fights, including the famous playwright Christopher Marlowe, who was killed in a brawl in 1593.

Outside the City walls, Shoreditch was home to the *Theatre* (1576) and the *Curtain* (1577) playhouses.

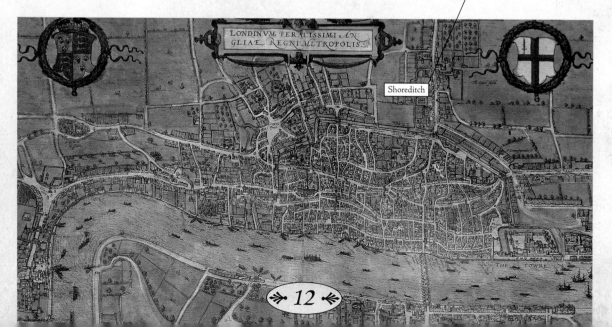

LONDINVM FERACISSIMI ANGLIAE REGNI METROPOLIS

Shoreditch

PLAGUE!

London was filthy, with rubbish lying in the streets and disease was a constant threat. London suffered from many **epidemics** of bubonic plague. This was a deadly disease that was spread by fleas. These fleas lived on the rats, who in turn lived among the mounds of rubbish.

Symptoms of the plague included aches and pains, a pink rash, high fever and terrible vomiting.

Victims usually died within 2–5 days. In the epidemic of 1592, many thousands of people died. The disease had an effect on the playhouses. When 30 people in London had the plague, the authorities shut all theatres fearing crowds would spread the infection.

This engraving shows the weekly plague burials that happened in London. Notice the skeleton ('death') visiting the City.

The London theatres

Before purpose-built theatres were built, the inns of London doubled up as theatres. The courtyards provided spaces for actors and audiences, and their narrow entrances allowed organisers to control access from the street.

Theatre-inns

The most famous theatre-inn was the *Black Bull* at Bishopsgate. In the 1580s, it was a favourite venue for the *Queen's Men*, so if Shakespeare did arrive in London with the troupe, he would have acted and possibly lodged there. The *Queen's Men* also used the *Bell* in Gracechurch Street and next door was the *Cross Keys*, where Shakespeare acted with the *Chamberlain's Men* in the 1590s.

The inns had galleries from which residents could watch the plays.

Purpose-built playhouses

Theatre-inns were small, so audience numbers had to be limited. Most theatres had a stage that was partially covered by a thatched roof held up by two pillars.

The stage extended into the uncovered area, which was surrounded by three floors of galleries for spectators. The stage had a trap door for special effects, such as ghosts or speedy exits and the stage roof had a machine room for winching actors through the air.

Theatres were also used as 'bear-pits'. Their circular or octagonal shape allowed for a circular pit where the animals, such as bears, fought.

THE GLOBE

Once the *Globe* theatre was re-built on Bankside, with its famous inscription, 'All the World's a stage', it could hold up to 3,300 spectators!

A sketch of the *Swan* theatre by the Dutch artist Arend van Buchell from 1596. It is the only drawing of an Elizabethan theatre that survives today.

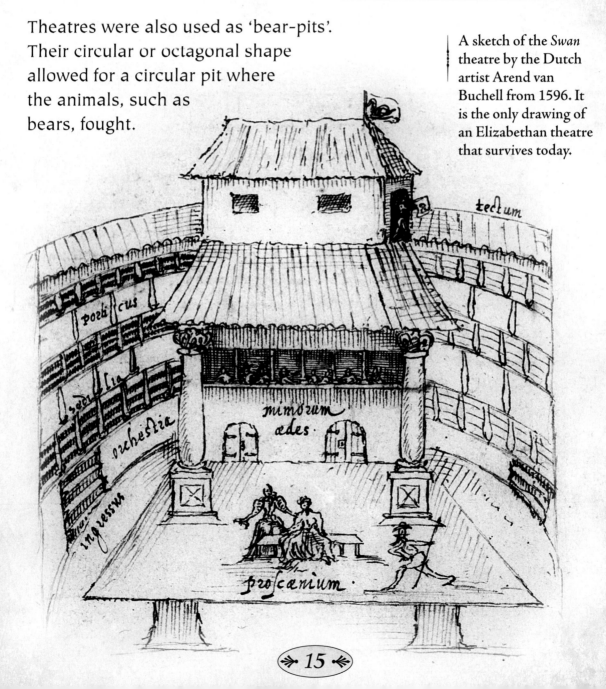

The players

In 1572, the queen's government passed a law that meant actors could only perform if they were sponsored by a respected and wealthy person. They also had to join a company or they could be imprisoned and **branded**.

The travelling companies

Shakespeare was an actor-member of a number of these troupes throughout his career. He probably began with the *Queen's Men*, joined the *Lord Strange's Men* and when Lord Strange died, joined the *Chamberlain's Men* in 1594. This troupe was named after Lord Hunsdon, the Lord Chamberlain.

Each troupe might contain up to 20 actors, which included a number of boys to play female roles. Women did not appear on stage at this time. A clown or fool was usually needed for 'comic relief'.

Learning lines

The actors worked very hard, having to learn their lines quickly, often in less than two weeks. This was difficult when they were learning the lines for more than one part.

Nathan Field (1586–1619) began as a child actor and was a principal actor in the same company as William Shakespeare.

ELIZABETH I

Elizabeth became Queen when her half-sister, Queen Mary I, died suddenly in 1558. Elizabeth ruled England for 45 years, from 1558 to 1603. It was a dramatic time and she had to cope with threats against her and her country from both home and abroad. Most famously, in 1588, the Spanish Armada (a huge **fleet** of warships) tried to **invade** England, but was defeated by the English **navy**.

Elizabeth loved being entertained and her court had a full programme of feasts, dances, music and plays. The Christmas festivities always included plays and the *Chamberlain's Men* were often 'commanded' to perform at the royal court.

The *Chamberlain's Men* performed many times at Elizabeth's court and she particularly liked one of Shakespeare's comedy characters, Sir John Falstaff. Here the players act out a comedy.

Getting noticed

Shakespeare's career as a playwright probably began in about 1590. The order in which he wrote his plays is not known, but experts believe the first ones were *Henry VI* (Parts 1-3), *Richard III* and *Titus Andronicus*. He also wrote some very popular poetry at this time.

Shakespeare attacked!

We know that Shakespeare had started writing plays because a pamphlet, which was published in 1592, severely attacked his work. A fellow playwright, Robert Greene, called Shakespeare an untrustworthy 'upstart crow, beautified with our feathers'. He then accused him of being an 'absolute Jack of all trades'. It's possible Greene was jealous of Shakespeare and could not believe a person without a university education had become so successful.

This is the home of the Earl of Southampton, Titchfield Abbey in Hampshire. Shakespeare may have been a guest while the plague ravaged London.

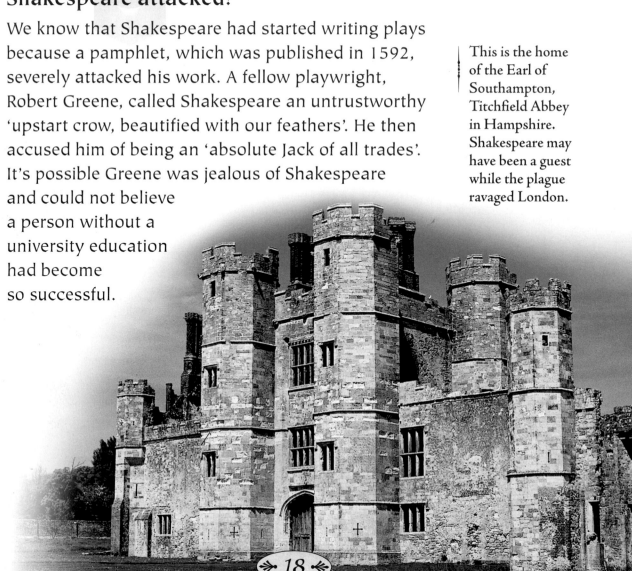

A poet

On 7th September 1592, London's theatres closed because of a serious outbreak of the plague. They remained shut for nearly two years. Some historians believe Shakespeare went abroad, perhaps to Italy during this time, while others think he returned home to his family in Stratford.

Henry Wriothesley, the 3rd Earl of Southampton, encouraged Shakespeare's writing and may have given him financial backing.

The Earl of Southampton

In April 1593, Shakespeare dedicated a poem, *Venus and Adonis*, to Henry Wriothesley, the Earl of Southampton. The poem was about love, beauty and death, and it was a great success. He followed it with another poem, *Lucrece*, also dedicated to Henry. Shakespeare was probably trying to get financial support from the Earl. It may have worked, for some people believe the Earl gave him a gift of £1,000 – a huge sum in those days!

In the 1590s, Shakespeare was also writing **sonnets**, 14-line poems. Not published until 1609, they contained many of Shakespeare's most famous lines. Sonnet 18 begins: 'Shall I compare thee to a Summer's day?' By 1596, Shakespeare was an accomplished poet, and success was soon to follow as a playwright, too.

Fame!

Shakespeare was in his thirties when he wrote some of the most famous plays in the world. It seemed that whatever he wrote – comedies, histories or **tragedies** – his popularity and reputation rapidly grew.

Plays and plots

Not all Shakespeare's plays were new. He often took an old play and revised it, changing the story and the characters. He borrowed plots, lines and names from many sources, particularly Roman literature. Other playwrights of the time, like Christopher Marlowe and Ben Jonson, did the same thing.

This habit of borrowing or recycling older plots and plays is a sign of the pressure playwrights were under to produce new work quickly. Shakespeare was a **shareholder** in the *Chamberlain's Men*.

This painting is thought to be quite a good likeness of Shakespeare.

As a shareholder, he had money invested in the troupe, so he had to come up with a steady stream of new plays to attract audiences if he was to get his money back and make any profit.

Success

In 1598, Shakespeare's success was recognised. The critic, Francis Meres, in his review *Wits Treasury* wrote, 'As Plautus and Seneca are accounted the best comedy and tragedy amongst the Romans so Shakespeare among the English is the most excellent, in both kinds for the stage. For comedy witness his *The Two Gentlemen of Verona*, his *Errors*, his *Love Labour's Lost…* for tragedy his *Richard II… Richard III… King John.'*

TRAGEDY!

Shakespeare's son, Hamnet died in August 1596 at just 11 years old. We don't know the cause of his death, but the plague was near Stratford that summer. In Shakespeare's play *King John* there are some lines that perhaps only a **grieving** parent could have written:

'Grief fills the room of my absent child, Lies in his bed, walking up and down with me, Puts on his pretty looks, repeats his words…'

A reconstruction of the *Swan* theatre on Bankside, showing the first act of Shakespeare's *Romeo and Juliet*.

A wealthy gentleman

Shakespeare may have returned to Stratford each year during **Lent**, when the theatres were closed. Perhaps also the death of his son, Hamnet persuaded him to spend more time with his family. In 1597, he bought New Place, the second largest house in Stratford for £60 and moved in with his family.

A man of property

Shakespeare bought more property in and around Stratford. These included cottages and barns, and Shakespeare began trading in corn, hay and malt. In 1602, he bought a large farm for £320. He received a good **income** in **rent** from these properties, ensuring the family's financial future was secure.

With the new *Globe* theatre ready by the summer of 1599, Shakespeare continued to produce crowd pleasers, such as *As You Like It*, *Twelfth Night*, and *Hamlet*, in which he played the ghost himself!

The house below (right) is on the site where the original New Place stood. The house was a sign of Shakespeare's increasing wealth.

PLOTTING AGAINST THE QUEEN

In February 1601, Shakespeare became dangerously involved in the politics of the day. The Earl of Essex was plotting against Queen Elizabeth I. He paid the *Chamberlain's Men* £2 to put on a public performance of *Richard II*. The play contained the overthrow and murder of a king and would have been a 'signal' for the rebellion against Queen Elizabeth. The uprising failed due to a lack of support, but the *Chamberlain's Men* were questioned about their part in it.

They were found innocent and on 22 February, the day Elizabeth signed the Earl's **death warrant**, the troupe performed for the Queen at Whitehall Palace.

If the rebellion had been successful, the Earl of Essex would have marched through London and stormed Whitehall Palace. It was Elizabeth's favourite residence.

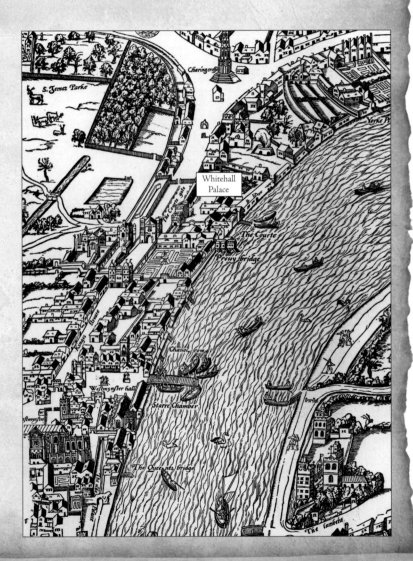

Shakespeare's last years

Queen Elizabeth I died in March 1603 and James I **succeeded** her. James also loved the theatre and he granted Shakespeare and his companions royal support. They became known as the *King's Men* and, between 1604 and 1605, they performed 11 times before the king.

Private grief, public success

Shakespeare continued to live modestly in London, lodging in a house in Silver Street. However, this was a sad time for Shakespeare as he lost his parents and, in 1607, both his brother Edmund and niece, Mary, died. In 1612, his brother Gilbert died, followed by Richard a year later. By 1613, six of Shakespeare's brothers and sisters had died.

Meanwhile, Shakespeare's career was thriving and, in 1608, permission was finally granted to open the *Blackfriars* theatre. Although smaller than the *Globe*, admission prices were higher. This was because it was an indoor theatre and more comfortable.

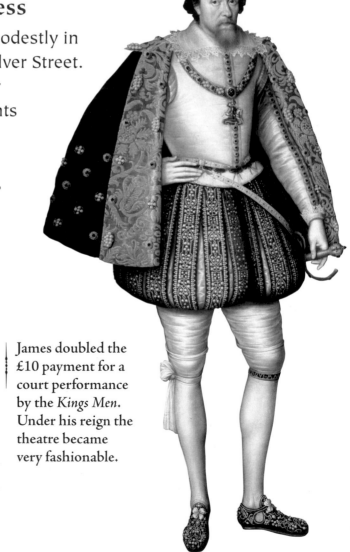

James doubled the £10 payment for a court performance by the *Kings Men*. Under his reign the theatre became very fashionable.

GOOD FREND FOR IESVS SAKE FORBEARE,
TO DIGG THE DVST ENCLOASED HEARE.
BLESE BE Y MAN Y SPARES THES STONES,
AND CVRST BE HE Y MOVES MY BONES.

There is a famous curse on Shakespeare's grave in Holy Trinity Church, Stratford, which you can see here. So far, no-one has dared to open it up!

Retirement

The *Globe* burned down in 1613. A spark from a cannon set the thatched roof on fire during a performance of *Henry VIII*.

Shakespeare retired to Stratford after the fire. He still visited London and saw his plays, *The Tempest* and *A Winter's Tale*, performed in front of the King.

LAST WILL AND TESTAMENT

In January 1616, Shakespeare made his **will**, famously giving 'My wife my second best bed'. This refers to their marital bed, for the 'best' bed was always kept for visitors. Although his daughter, Susanna, received most of his property, his wife, Anne, would have been well-provided for.

On 23 April 1616, Shakespeare died aged 52. We don't know the cause of his death, but ill-health might have encouraged him to write his will. As he wrote in *The Tempest*:

'Our revels are now ended…
And our little life
Is rounded with a sleep.'

Why is William Shakespeare important today?

After Shakespeare's death in 1616, two acting companions, John Heminges and Henry Condell, spent years collecting together his scripts. In 1623, they published the *First Folio*, containing 36 plays. Most have never gone out of fashion, perhaps because they are concerned with situations everyone recognises, such as teenage love and differences in social background.

Influence

William's work has had a huge influence on the world of literature, art, music and film. Composers such as Mendelssohn and Tchaikovsky wrote music to *A Midsummer Night's Dream* and *Romeo and Juliet*. The English **Pre-Raphaelite** artists based many of their paintings on Shakespeare's plays.

Claire Danes and Leonardo DiCaprio acted as the main characters in the 1996 film version of *Romeo and Juliet*.

John Millais' painting, *Ophelia* is still one of the most popular attractions in Tate Britain today. The Victorians loved Shakespeare's tragedies and they deeply influenced novelists such as Thomas Hardy, Charles Dickens and, in America, Herman Melville.

Shakespeare and the cinema

The play *Hamlet* was first filmed 1913. Cinema has often changed or updated Shakespeare's popular plays. *Romeo and Juliet* became gangland New York in *West Side Story* and the 1996 Leonardo DiCaprio version was completely modernised. Japanese director Kurosawa placed both the stories of *Macbeth* and *King Lear* amongst Samurai warriors in medieval Japan.

A tourist attraction

Today, Stratford is visited frequently by admirers of Shakespeare wishing to learn more about his life. The impressive *Royal Shakespeare* theatre is on the banks of the River Avon. In London, the *Globe* has been re-constructed near its original site, and regularly performs Shakespeare's plays.

The *Globe* theatre was rebuilt in 1997. It was the first thatched building to be built in London since the Great Fire of London in 1666!

A walk through the life of William Shakespeare

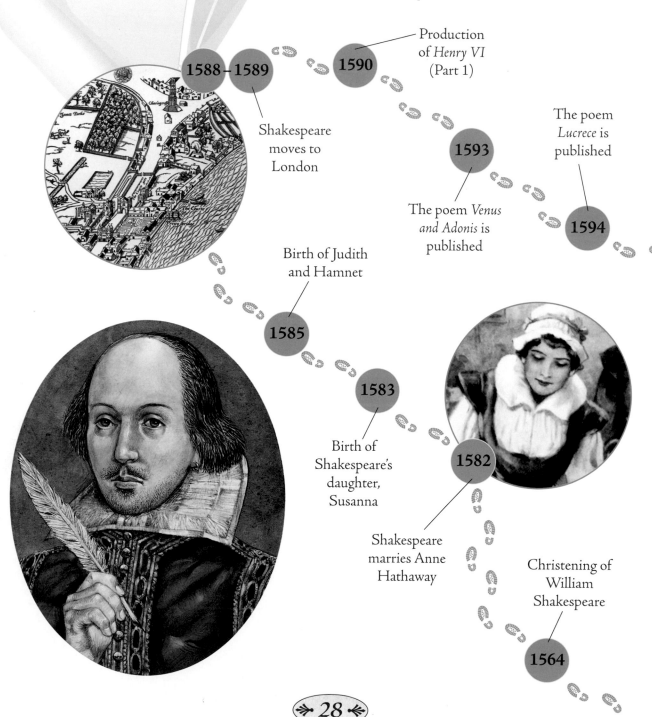

1588–1589

Shakespeare moves to London

1590 — Production of *Henry VI* (Part 1)

1593

The poem *Venus and Adonis* is published

The poem *Lucrece* is published

1594

Birth of Judith and Hamnet

1585

1583

Birth of Shakespeare's daughter, Susanna

1582

Shakespeare marries Anne Hathaway

Christening of William Shakespeare

1564

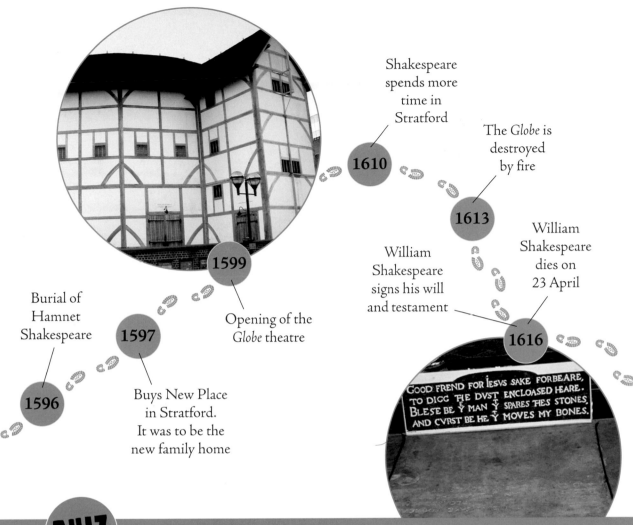

Shakespeare spends more time in Stratford

1610

The *Globe* is destroyed by fire

1613

William Shakespeare dies on 23 April

Burial of Hamnet Shakespeare

William Shakespeare signs his will and testament

1599

Opening of the *Globe* theatre

1597

1596

1616

Buys New Place in Stratford. It was to be the new family home

GOOD FREND FOR IESVS SAKE FORBEARE,
TO DIGG THE DVST ENCLOASED HEARE.
BLESE BE Y MAN y SPARES THES STONES,
AND CVRST BE HE Y MOVES MY BONES.

QUIZ

WHAT DO YOU KNOW ABOUT SHAKESPEARE?

1. As a baby, what chance did Shakespeare have of surviving in the 16th century?

2. How old was Shakespeare when he married, and how old was his bride, Anne Hathaway?

3. Where might Shakespeare's interest in theatre have come from?

4. Name the two poems that Shakespeare wrote in 1593–94.

5. Shakespeare's plays are divided up into three kinds of subject matter – what are they?

Answers: 1. He had a one in five chance of survival **2.** Shakespeare was 18 and Anne was 26 **3.** From witnessing the acting troupes visiting Stratford-Upon-Avon during his childhood **4.** *Venus and Adonis* and *Lucrece* **5.** Comedies, tragedies and histories

Cross-curricular links

Use this topic web to explore the life of William Shakespeare in different areas of your curriculum.

HISTORY
Elizabethan England
- The Spanish Armada
- Religious persecution
- Plots and rebellions
- Plague and hygiene

GEOGRAPHY
- Stratford-upon-Avon
- County of Warwickshire
- London – City/Shoreditch/Bankside/'theatre land'
- Elizabethan trade routes

MUSIC
- Music in Shakespeare – songs from the plays
- Elizabethan composer, William Byrd
- Music inspired by the plays – Mendelsohnn, Tchaikovsky, Verdi

WILLIAM SHAKESPEARE

ART
- Shakespeare in painting
- Joshua Reynolds
- William Blake
- Henry Fuseli
- The Pre-Raphaelite Brotherhood – Millais, Holman-Hunt, Rossetti

DRAMA
- Elizabethan theatre - layout
- The Globe
- Actors and Acting

ENGLISH
- The Sonnets
- Poetry
- The Plays – 'Histories, Comedies and Tragedies'
- Stories from Shakespeare

Glossary

alderman A member of a town council.

apprentice A young person who learns a trade from someone.

branded To be burned with a red-hot iron on the skin.

Catechism A book to be learned containing questions and answers about the Christian faith.

City fathers The Lord Mayor and senior aldermen who ran the City of London.

death warrant An order for someone to be killed.

epidemics The spread of a disease.

fleet A large group of ships.

galleries Balconies that provide a good view.

grammar school A school for older children, that concentrated on teaching Latin.

grieving When a person is sad because a loved one has died.

income The money someone earns.

inn-yards The courtyard of an inn or public house.

invade To send troops to take over another country.

Lent In the Christian faith, the forty–day period leading up to Easter.

market town A settlement where locally produced goods are bought and sold.

navy The ships and sailors that defend a country.

petty school A first school for young children.

plague A dangerous disease.

playwrights People who write plays.

Pre-Raphaelite A group of painters in Victorian Britain who painted in a very realistic way.

prosperity Success and wealth.

rent Money paid for the occupation of a house or land.

sewage Human waste.

shareholder Someone who invests money in a company and is entitled to a share of the profits.

sonnets 14-line poems.

succeeded To take over the rule of a country.

traded To buy and sell goods.

tragedies Plays that have a serious or unhappy ending.

troupe A group of travelling actors.

will A legal list of possessions given away by someone after their death.

Index

Numbers in **bold** refer to photographs or illustrations.

Further Information

More books to read

Be a History Detective: Tudor Theatre by Katie Dicker (Wayland, 2009)

Famous People, Famous Lives: William Shakespeare by Emma Fischel (Franklin Watts, 2002)

Tudor Life: Entertainment by Nicola Barber (Wayland, 2009)

Places to visit

- Stratford-Upon-Avon
- *Globe* theatre, London
- *Royal Shakespeare Company*, Stratford-Upon-Avon

Useful websites

www.william-shakespeare.info/site-map.htm
A detailed website about Shakespeare's life.

www.stratford-upon-avon.co.uk/
Information about Shakespeare's birthplace.

www.shakespeares-globe.org/
The website of the *Globe* theatre in London. Find out about the original theatre and which of Shakespeare's plays are being shown at the theatre today.